Saint Patrick's Day

Buddy BOOKS
Holidays

ABDO
Publishing Company

A Buddy Book
by
Julie Murray

VISIT US AT
www.abdopublishing.com

Published by ABDO Publishing Company, 8000 West 78th Street, Edina, Minnesota 55439.

Copyright © 2012 by Abdo Consulting Group, Inc. International copyrights reserved in all countries. No part of this book may be reproduced in any form without written permission from the publisher. Buddy Books™ is a trademark and logo of ABDO Publishing Company.

Printed in the United States of America, North Mankato, Minnesota.
052011
092011

 PRINTED ON RECYCLED PAPER

Coordinating Series Editor: Rochelle Baltzer
Editor: Sarah Tieck
Contributing Editors: Megan M. Gunderson, BreAnn Rumsch, Marcia Zappa
Graphic Design: Denise Esner
Cover Photograph: *AP Photo*: Graham Hughes, CP.
Interior Photographs/Illustrations: *AP Photo*: AP Photo (p. 21), Mary Altaffer (p. 9), Ron Edmonds (p. 13), Shawn Gust/Coeur d'Alene Press (p. 17), Peter Morrison (p. 5); *Getty Images*: Archive Photos (p. 7); *iStockphoto*: ©iStockphoto.com/LauriPatterson (p. 19), ©iStockphoto.com/sbossert (p. 19); *Michael David Novak* (pp. 11, 15, 20); *Shutterstock*: Ambient Ideas (p. 6), Thomas Barrat (p. 13), Joerg Beuge (p. 19), sepavo (p. 8), Matt Smith (p. 22).

Library of Congress Cataloging-in-Publication Data

Murray, Julie, 1969-
  Saint Patrick's Day / Julie Murray.
     p. cm. -- (Holidays)
  ISBN 978-1-61783-042-6
  1. Saint Patrick's Day--Juvenile literature. I. Title.
GT4995.P3M87 2012
394.262--dc22
                          2011002291

Table of Contents

What Is Saint Patrick's Day?

Saint Patrick's Day happens every year on March 17. On this day, people remember Saint Patrick. He was a special saint in Ireland.

On Saint Patrick's Day, some people pray or attend church. Others **celebrate** Irish **culture**. They go to parades and parties. Family and friends share food and fun.

Saint Patrick's Day was first a church holiday. For many people, it is now a celebration of Irish food, drink, and music.

N
W—E
S

Atlantic Ocean

North Sea

IRELAND

UNITED KINGDOM

Early Celebrations

No one knows for sure when Saint Patrick's Day started. But, Irish people started honoring Saint Patrick after his death in AD 461.

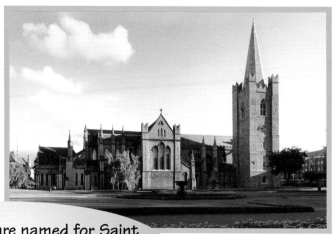

Many churches are named for Saint Patrick. This includes Saint Patrick's Cathedral in Ireland's capital, Dublin.

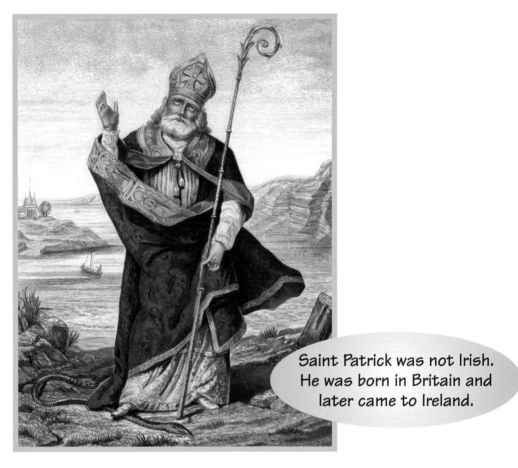

Saint Patrick was not Irish. He was born in Britain and later came to Ireland.

Saint Patrick is famous for bringing **Christianity** to Ireland. Before this, most Irish people were **Celtic pagans**. Saint Patrick's teachings changed their faith and ideas.

For many years, people in Ireland went to church on Saint Patrick's Day. Over time, Saint Patrick's Day **celebrations** grew and spread to other parts of the world.

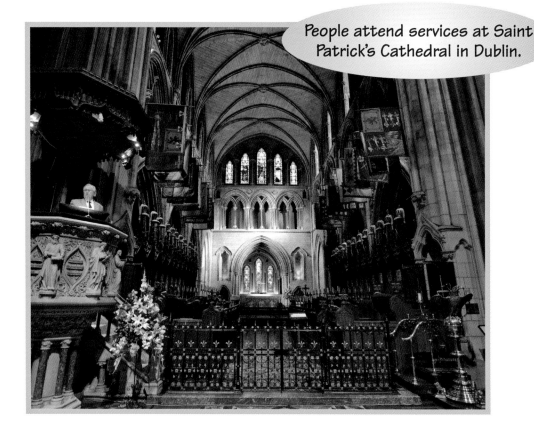

People attend services at Saint Patrick's Cathedral in Dublin.

In New York City, Irish dances were part of the Saint Patrick's Day Parade in 2010.

The largest Saint Patrick's Day **celebrations** happen where many Irish people live. One of the first was in 1737 in Boston, Massachusetts. New York City, New York, held its first Saint Patrick's Day parade in 1762.

Teaching Tool

Holidays often have special **symbols**. The shamrock is one Saint Patrick's Day symbol. Several types of small plants with three leaves are called shamrocks. They are common in Ireland.

Some say Saint Patrick used the shamrock to teach **Christianity**. The plant's three leaves stood for the Trinity. In Christianity, the Trinity is the three forms of God. These are the Father, the Son, and the Holy Spirit.

Today, the shamrock is a symbol of Ireland.

Feeling Green

When people think of Saint Patrick's Day, they think of the color green. This is because Ireland is known for being green. It gets lots of rain, so plants grow almost everywhere! Also, green is part of Ireland's flag.

People often wear green on Saint Patrick's Day. In many cities, people serve green drinks or foods. And in Chicago, Illinois, the Chicago River is dyed green!

On Saint Patrick's Day in 2009,
the White House fountains were dyed green.
This was First Lady Michelle Obama's idea.
She grew up in Chicago, which is known for
celebrating the holiday.

Today, the Chicago River is
dyed green for a couple of hours on
Saint Patrick's Day. In the 1960s, the
river stayed green for a week!

Irish Music

Music is an important part of Irish **culture**. There is often live music in Irish pubs. Pubs are public houses that serve drinks and meals.

People gather in Irish pubs on Saint Patrick's Day. There, they may watch dancers and singers. They may also listen to people play instruments. These include accordions, pipes, and guitars.

Irish pubs are full of fun and life. Sometimes musicians even move throughout the crowd. Temple Bar (*above*) is a famous pub in Dublin.

Eat and Drink

Saint Patrick's Day takes place during Lent. Over these 40 days, most **Christians** prepare for a special holiday called Easter.

One way they prepare is by not eating certain foods. For some, Saint Patrick's Day can be a break to eat whatever they want.

During Lent, many people avoid eating meat on special days. But sometimes on Saint Patrick's Day, they can enjoy a special feast.

Today, many people enjoy special food on Saint Patrick's Day. In the United States, corned beef and cabbage is one **traditional** meal. Irish **immigrants** made this meal popular.

In Ireland, people may eat other traditional foods. These include Irish stew, shepherd's pie, and Irish bacon and cabbage.

Corned beef and cabbage

Irish stew

Shepherd's pie

Saint Patrick's Day Today

Today, Saint Patrick's Day is mainly a **celebration** of Irish **culture**. One of the largest events is in Dublin, Ireland. It takes place on and around March 17.

The Liffey, or Ha'penny, Bridge crosses the River Liffey in downtown Dublin. Several Saint Patrick's Day events happen there.

On Saint Patrick's Day, people fill the streets of Dublin!

People from around the world gather in Dublin to **celebrate**. They watch a parade, listen to Irish music, and visit Saint Patrick's Cathedral. They also learn about Saint Patrick, who changed the history of Ireland.

Tricky Leprechauns

Saint Patrick's Day makes people think of leprechauns (LEHP-ruh-kahns). In Irish stories, leprechauns are little old men known for making shoes. Some people believe these fairies have hidden pots of gold.

It is said that if you capture one, you might get his pot of gold. But, most leprechauns are very tricky and usually escape!

Leprechauns are a symbol of Irish culture.

Important Words

celebrate to observe a holiday with special events. These events are known as celebrations.

Celtic (KEHL-tihk) relating to people who lived about 2,000 years ago in many countries of western Europe.

Christianity (krihs-chee-A-nuh-tee) a religion that follows the teachings of Jesus Christ. Christians are people who practice Christianity.

culture the arts, beliefs, and ways of life of a group of people.

immigrant someone who has left his or her home and settled in a new country.

pagan a person who worships many gods or goddesses.

symbol (SIHM-buhl) an object or mark that stands for an idea.

traditional (truh-DIHSH-nuhl) relating to beliefs, customs, and stories handed down from older people to younger people.

Web Sites

To learn more about Saint Patrick's Day,

visit ABDO Publishing Company online. Web sites about Saint Patrick's Day are featured on our Book Links page. These links are routinely monitored and updated to provide the most current information available.

www.abdopublishing.com

Index